Philips

TALKABOUT
Growing

Text: Henry Pluckrose
Photography: Chris Fairclough

Franklin Watts
London/New York/Sydney/Toronto

© 1988 Franklin Watts

First published in Great Britain by

Franklin Watts
12a Golden Square
London W1

First published in the USA by

Franklin Watts Inc
387 Park Avenue South
New York 10016

ISBN: UK edition 0 86313 505 6

ISBN: US edition 0–531–10454–0
Library of Congress
Catalog Card No: 87–50587

Editor: Ruth Thomson
Design: Edward Kinsey

Additional photographs: Heather Angel, NHPA, Zefa

Typesetting: Keyspools Ltd
Printed in Hong Kong

About this book

This book has been written for young children—in the playgroup, school and at home.

Its aim is to increase children's awareness of the world around them and to promote thought and discussion about topics of scientific interest.

The book draws on examples from a child's own environment. The activities and experiments suggested are simple enough for children to conduct themselves, with only a little help from an adult, using objects and materials which will be familiar to them.

Children will gain most from the book if the book is used together with practical activities. Such experiences will help to consolidate knowledge and also suggest new ideas for further exploration and experimentation.

The themes explored in this book include:

Growing things increase in size and weight.
Growing things look different when fully grown.
Growing things need food and water.
Growing things become old.

You were tiny
when you were born.

Now you have grown
much bigger
and taller.

You will grow up
and perhaps have a family
of your own.

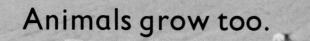

Animals grow too.

These sheep . . .

were once lambs.

This lion . . .

was once a cub.

Some things look quite different when they are fully grown.

This butterfly . . .

was once a caterpillar.

These sunflowers . . .

have grown
from seeds.

What do you think
is hatching from this egg?

What do you think is growing inside these eggs?

Without food,
we would not grow.
What food do you like
best of all?

Animals and birds need food too.
What is this bird eating?

Plants need the soil,
which contains their food.

They also must have water, and the light and warmth of the sun.

Plants take in food and water
through their roots
and sunlight through their leaves.

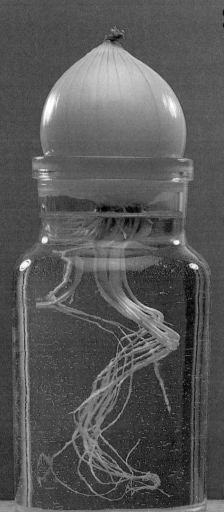

Some bulbs will grow
in water.

This onion
has grown roots.
To grow, it is using up
food stored in the bulb.

In spring,
many trees
have blossom.

This is
apple blossom.

When the blossom fades, the apples form.

In autumn,
the apples are harvested.
Apples are the fruit of the tree.

Cut open
an apple.
What can
you see?

Each of
these seeds
could grow
into a tree!

Growing
means changing
shape
and size.

How can you tell
you have grown?

How can you measure your growth?

You will grow old.

All people change
as they grow older.